IMAGES
of America

JACKSON HOLE

ON THE COVER: The residents and guests of the Hotel Jackson took a pause long enough for Stephen Leek to capture this early image. The mud and muck of the street show the need for elevated boardwalk sidewalks. Snow King Mountain rises in the background, denuded of timber after a recent fire. (Courtesy of the Wyoming State Archives.)

IMAGES
of America

JACKSON HOLE

Scott Morris

ARCADIA
PUBLISHING

Published by Arcadia Publishing
Charleston, South Carolina

Printed in the United States of America

Library of Congress Control Number: 2023944337

For all general information, please contact Arcadia Publishing:
Telephone 843-853-2070
Fax 843-853-0044
E-mail sales@arcadiapublishing.com

Visit us on the Internet at www.arcadiapublishing.com

Dedicated to the Wyoming landscape, which bears so much of humans' follies and gives so much back in return. And to Grace, who does the same for me.

CONTENTS

ACKNOWLEDGMENTS

Many thanks to the staff at the Wyoming State Archives, the American Heritage Center at the University of Wyoming, and the Marriott Library at the University of Utah. Thanks are also due to anyone who cares about Wyoming history and takes a moment to consider how the past has given us the world we inhabit today.

INTRODUCTION

The valleys, ranges, rivers, and sagebrush ecosystems that would become Jackson Hole, Wyoming, have a long history of indigenous lifeways. While there will always be less known about the deep past than more recent chapters, archaeological evidence suggests that people have used these landscapes for at least 11,000 years. Dr. Gary Wright of the University at Albany theorized that Early Archaic people spent the summer moving through the valley, increasing in elevation as resources became seasonally available. Wright's *People of the High Country: Jackson Hole before the Settlers* combined archaeological and ethnohistorical methods to study a millennia-long lifeway that combined a reliance on root crops, summer fishing, and winter hunting. Evidence of roasting pits and fishing camps on the shores of Jackson, which were inundated in 1916 when the dam raised the level of the lake, support this view. Other sites, including one near Black Tail Butte on the Elk Refuge and another south of town at the mouth of Game Creek, all suggest a vibrant precontact life. Archeologists have looked at fishing net weights, mano and metate grinding stones, steatite bowls, hammer stones, and projectile points in order to try and get a glimpse into this ancient Jackson.

This cultural complex may have been upset several hundred years ago when Numic speakers, the ancestors of today's Shoshones, migrated in from the southwest. Power hierarchies, migratory routes, and socioeconomic lifeways would have been further disrupted when these groups obtained horses from the Spanish settlements to the south by way of more proximate neighbors. Regardless, Jackson Hole likely remained a borderland, a place where cultures melded and came to accommodations and where no one group exercised complete control. The historic groups that later generations of settlers would interact with all competed for influence and access to the resources of the high country. "The Teton region was a crossroads," explains writer Earle Layser, "a place where the territories of the Absaroka, Blackfoot, and Shoshone people converged."

Before the arrival of the horse, the Absaroka (also known as the Crow people) likely held the balance of power, though this was upset when the Shoshones and Blackfoot built up their herds and the Shoshones in particular positioned themselves in the middle of flows of horses to the north out of Spanish New Mexico and the flow of guns and other manufactured goods from Anglo-America to the east and Franco-America to the northeast. Washakie's band of Eastern Shoshone, well known to American settlers and government officials and valued for their pro-American and pro-assimilationist attitudes, were known to camp and hunt in Jackson Hole and the Teton Valley since at least the 1850s, no doubt a practice already generations old by that point. But as treaties began to be signed and Native people were pushed onto tightly defined reservation homelands, Native economies that relied on mobility in order to exploit seasonally available resources began to falter. The Fort Bridger Treaty of 1868 encouraged the Shoshone-Bannocks to stay around Fort Hall and pushed the Eastern Shoshone down into the lower Wind River Country, and the Fort Laramie Treaty of 1870 coerced the Absaroka onto the Crow Reservation in southern Montana. Add to this the demographic collapse resulting from virgin soil epidemics and the violence of settler colonialism, and the late 19th century was a trying time for the Native people of Wyoming. In

1879, the last of the Mountain Shoshone were forcibly removed from the Native homelands now being called Yellowstone National Park.

Native history in the Jackson region does not end here, as Indigenous people continued to cocreate cultural and ecological landscapes in the 20th and 21st centuries. But beginning in the 19th century, new generations of Euro-Americans would signal dramatic change for those cultural and ecological landscapes. Small parties of fur trappers paddling upstream on the tributaries of the Missouri began to introduce ideas of commodity capitalism, incorporating the region's resources into a global economic system. The Rocky Mountain fur trade only lasted a generation before becoming a victim to its own success, with trapped-out river systems and the resulting environmental degradation. But others would come after them, starting with a generation of government explorers and mapmakers who would also incorporate Jackson Hole into a larger national project. Like the economic linkages of the fur trade, this political incorporation would come with some turbulence.

While there was never any large-scale conflict between the Union and Confederacy in the Far West, the Civil War would dramatically reshape life there. New technologies, such as the transcontinental railroad, the freighting and stage coach companies that would extend its reach, the telegraph, barbed wire, new firearm technologies, and other developments, made settlement possible in new regions, even profitable in some. It also added a new scale of violence, especially for the region's Native people, as professional federal troops were sent back east and they were replaced with irregular volunteers from California and other roughneck societies of the West. The Bear River Massacre, the Sand Creek Massacre, and the Powder River Invasion all followed in quick succession.

The Civil War also catalyzed the deployment of new mining technology, which was brought into new regions by a generation of prospectors in search of the next bonanza. These miners explored new valleys the same way that fur trappers did, following the watercourse drainages up into the alpine heights.

The first concerted effort to judge Jackson Hole's mineral potential was led by Walter DeLacy in August 1863, when he led his so-called "40 thieves" up into Jackson Hole via the lower Snake River Canyon. These men were those who arrived too late to the strike earlier that year at Alder Gulch, Montana, and elected DeLacy as the man to lead them to a new bonanza. Panning the waters of the Snake as they traveled the length of the valley, by Jackson Lake they had not found anything suggesting golden riches. Splitting into two groups, half retreated south the way they had come, and another group ventured north into the Yellowstone Country. DeLacy's 40 thieves found no Euro-American homesteads or Native villages in Jackson Hole, suggesting that it had been largely ignored in the three decades since the Rocky Mountain fur trade had sputtered out. Another party of prospectors passed through Jackson Hole the next year, but they also did not find enough to elicit much interest.

Fast forward three decades to 1895, and there were more than a hundred men working placer mines around Crystal Creek, a tributary of the Gros Ventre River to the south of Jackson Hole. A ball machine from this era, which was used for smashing and grinding ores, is still visible on Crystal Creek. The limited success at the Crystal Creek diggings led to the 1889 construction of the first sawmill in the area by the Whetstone Mining Company. The district failed to supply the riches that boosters had imagined, and the sawmill was shuttered by 1897.

The fur trappers, gold prospectors, and government men had come and gone from the valley that would become Jackson Hole. Some, such as Beaver Dick, stuck around for longer than the others, etching out a living between trapping, hunting, and guiding since at least the middle of the Civil War. In 1876, Lt. Gustaves Doane, on his ill-fated winter march, found a man named John Pierce living in a makeshift cabin.

The date given in most stories about the founding of Jackson is 1884, when John Holland, Johnny Carnes, and Millie Sorelle (Carnes's wife of Native ancestry) horse packed some basic agricultural equipment into the southern part of Jackson Hole. But this is an arbitrary if not capricious beginning point, revealing little except American society's privileged opinion of agriculture over other lifeways and the persistent erasure of Native history. Both Carnes and Holland had been spending time in the valley since at least 1877 and had filed paperwork for the appropriation of water in 1883. At the same time, they maintained a herd of about a hundred cattle on the grasses of the valley's floor. Perhaps a better starting line for Jackson is the appropriation of water and the introduction of domesticated grazers.

Jackson's Euro-American settlement expanded with the 1889 arrival of Nick Wilson. Wilson had led a storied life, from when he ran away as a boy to live with Washakie's band of Shoshones to careers as a Pony Express rider, an Army scout, and an Overland Stage driver. Wilson embodied the chapters of Western history that have since become mythologized into a vision of the Old West. But all this was behind him when he crested Teton Pass in the fall of 1889 at the head of six wagons, five families of Mormon settlers, and herds of domesticated livestock. The settlement flourished, and two years later, Effie Jane Wilson became the first Euro-American child born in the valley. The Wilson clan and "Uncle Nick" became a natural feature of the valley and regaled later settlers with stories from his youth and adventures.

Jackson began earning a reputation for lawlessness with the residence of Teton Jackson and his gang of outlaws. Jackson was too far from the regional cattle trails to be much more than a winter hideout for two-bit cattle rustlers, but Teton Jackson's adoption of the regional name imprinted an association between these mountain valleys and the freedom from justice that isolated frontier towns could provide. The Wyoming Territory was organized in 1868, but even after territorial institutions were stood up, the law officer closest to Jackson was in Evanston, a 250-mile horseback ride away. This effectively put Jackson beyond the reach of the law, especially when winter conditions closed the passes into and out of the valley. A predictable volley of gunfire resulted, with much of 19th-century Jackson history being a story of guys killing each other for a variety of reasons. Despite this violence, early Jackson was very diverse, with the Native people and Anglo Americans one might expect but also Swiss, Germans, an Austrian, and even a few bachelors from Holland.

One of the more shameful incidents of Jackson history was the misnamed "Indian War of 1895." It is an episode that illustrated the violent nature of life on the Wyoming frontier in the late 19th century and the doggedness with which projects of settler colonialism dispossess Native people of their rights, their land, and their lives. Article Four of the Fort Bridger Treaty of 1868 specifically protects the right of Native people to exercise their traditional hunting practices on federal land. But the arrival of market hunters in the 1880s and 1890s had devastated the wildlife populations that Native people and early settlers relied on, leading to more conflict between these parties over diminishing resources. An effective demonstration of the animosity and approbation at play in the conflict is an 1892 article written by Theodore Roosevelt that blamed Indians for the declining stock of large animals.

But the Euro-American settlers were upset about Native people exercising their hunting rights nearby, especially as elk herds began to decline in the last decade of the 19th century. In July 1895, a posse of 27 men arrested a party of Bannocks ostensibly for violating state game laws, though this may have been the wrong group of Natives. What happened on the march back to town is hazy, but the posse began loading their rifles, and some of the Native people escaped. When the scuffle was over, a blind old Bannock man lay on the ground with four bullet holes in his back. Some reports feature a missing Bannock baby, and others have an Indian child taken and adopted into a white family.

Fearing retaliatory attacks, the settlers of Jackson "forted up" at a few strategic ranches, but no attack came. Meanwhile, rumor snowballed into misinformation, with a *New York Times* headline on July 27, 1895, reporting on a nonexistent Indian attack that killed every settler within riding distance of Jackson. Local and federal authorities responded to pleas for help with a posse riding over from Lander and the 9th Cavalry "Buffalo Soldiers" dispatched from Fort Robinson, Nebraska.

The false news was explained away as, in the words of historian Robert Betts, "manufactured by some of the settlers as part of a deliberate scheme to drive the Indians once and for all from what they considered to be their legitimate hunting grounds in the valley." Betts comments on the racial ironies at play, writing, "If the Indians had chosen a fight and a battle with the cavalry had taken place, it would have been a scene which, as the saying goes, could have happened only in America—members of the white race being defended from members of the red race by members of still another race, for most of the cavalry troopers who were sent to Jackson Hole were black."

It is important to note that the settlers' illegal and murderous actions in 1895 were successful—they extinguished, by force, Native peoples' treaty-protected hunting rights. This precedent was later enshrined in a Supreme Court decision that allowed state hunting laws to supersede the protections of treaties.

By tracing the actions of Native people, fur trappers, gold prospectors, and early settlers, this introduction has brought us from the Jackson Hole of the 19th century to the dawn of the 20th. It has also situated the valley of Jackson Hole in a broader regional context and what would become Jackson, Wyoming, within its namesake valley.

One

Fur Trappers and Government Explorers

John Colter may have visited Jackson Hole in 1807 or 1808, which would mark, if true, the first Euro-American entrance into the valley. He was a member of the Lewis and Clark Expedition who, when descending the Missouri, was confronted with two men headed upstream to trap beaver, and he turned around and headed back into the mountains. Opinions differ on whether or not Colter made it to Yellowstone, which reminded Americans of the "Colter's Hell" story of geysers and bubbling pots, with most contemporary opinion suggesting he likely made it as far as the Shoshone River, near today's Cody, Wyoming.

Historian Robert Betts has called Jackson Hole a crossroads of the fur trade from the beginning. In the fall of 1810, a few men working for Andrew Henry, probably under the leadership of John Dougherty, made a fall and winter hunt in the drainages above the future Jackson. The next year saw a crossing in Teton Pass and out over Togwotee Pass of three more of Henry's trappers. These men were also talked into returning upcountry by trappers of a competing firm. Led by Wilson Price Hunt, they went over Union Pass, swung through bison country to the south to get food, and then entered Jackson Hole via the Hoback River. After exploring the lower part of the valley, where the town now sits, Hunt detached four trappers to stay behind and further explore the fur-bearing potential of the region. These four trappers spent the winter moving up and down the Snake River before bugging out over Teton Pass in the spring of 1812 toward Fort Astoria on the Pacific Coast. That fall, trappers working under John Jacob Astor again entered Jackson Hole via Teton Pass, went out the Hoback River, and then made the first Euro-American crossing of South Pass, the route that would prove to be the lynchpin of the Overland Trails.

The "high age" of the Rocky Mountain fur trade began when William Henry Ashley and his partners and employees started sending expeditions up the Missouri in the spring of 1822 and built a fort at the mouth of the Yellowstone. Despite their efforts, the Arikaras and other Missouri River tribes controlled how and when American trappers could use the river, all while attempting to shape trade to benefit them against their rivals and enemies. Ashley's men proceeded overland to the mountains, in the process reinventing the industry with seasonal rendezvous that could keep the men in the mountains year-round, transport supplies and furs in one seasonal move, and more effectively control supply, demand, and labor.

Six American trappers under the leadership of Jed Smith trapped their way up Jackson Hole and exited via Conant Pass. In what is today Montana, they bumped into the Hudson Bay Company, exacerbating a corporate rivalry couched in a larger geopolitical struggle between the United States and Great Britain over the Oregon Territory. The British attempted to create a "fur desert" to keep the Americans from moving west. But they did not stop coming, and in the late 1820s, Davy Jackson lent the valley his name through repeated trapping expeditions. One estimate by historian Robert Betts puts the number of trapping parties in the valley between 1829 and 1840 at 30, "Enough to say that Jackson Hole was the main arena of the fur trade."

Multiple rendezvous were held in Pierre's Hole, across the Tetons, in the 1830s, which brought lots of famous trappers through the Hole, including Jim Bridger, Joe Meek, "Broken Hand" Fitzpatrick, Osborne Russell, Jed Smith, and William Sublette. These trappers participated in the 1832 "Battle of Pierre's Hole," which was the largest-yet spasm of violence between Americans and Natives, a sign of wider conflicts to come.

The Rocky Mountain fur trade declined after 1840, a victim of its own success, competition-fueled over-trapping, and changes in hat fashion. Trappers would still work the gullies and valleys of Jackson Hole, but the days of a full-time fur brigade and its yearly rendezvous were over. The valley would go mostly unvisited for a generation, all while war with Mexico was won and California, Oregon, and Utah were settled.

The man who would make the biggest mark on expanding federal authority into Jackson Hole was geologist Ferdidand Harden, a doctor of geology. The Sioux people called him Man-Who-Picks-Up-Rocks-Running. He first visited the region as a member of the 1860 Reynolds Expedition, which was guided by an aging Jim Bridger. After exploring and naming Union Pass, the Reynolds team was forced to descend into Jackson Hole by snow and challenging terrain. They found an engorged Snake River that took three days to cross and the life of one man.

Hayden's leadership of three expeditions in 1872, 1877, and 1878 dramatically increased Euro-American understanding of the valleys and mountains surrounding Jackson Hole. Perhaps his biggest contribution was an invitation to photographer W.H. Jackson and painter Thomas Moran, who brought Western landscapes back to Eastern audiences. This public relations push is credited with inspiring Congress to declare the first-ever national park.

Hayden's first expedition was followed by the 1873 Jones Expedition, which explored the newly created Yellowstone National Park in order to build a road through it. Abandoned by their Shoshone guides, they groped their way south and east into Jackson Hole and over Togwotee Pass, naming it for the only guide who had not left them.

Things would get even worse for the members of Lt. Gustaves Doane's team in the winter of 1876. Doane had led the Army escort of the 1870 Washburn Expedition and was also instrumental in the declaration of Yellowstone National Park. They entered Jackson Hole in late December after beating a retreat out of the Yellowstone high country. Surviving by this point on horse meat and fish, they found a settler named John Pierce living in the valley who gave them some elk meat. They tried to leave by boating down the Snake but capsized in the freezing rapids.

This painting by William Henry Jackson depicts the fur trappers' rendezvous of 1837. That year, the gathering was in the Green River Valley, near today's Daniel, Wyoming. This favored spot was just south of Jackson Hole but was convenient for trappers working the region. Trappers were constantly traversing the valley going to and from their hunting grounds or these gatherings, where they would exchange their year's catch of furs for the supplies they would need to survive until the next season. (Courtesy of the Wyoming State Archives.)

JOHN COLTER
1807 - 1957

John Colter may have been the first Euro-American to visit what is now Wyoming, three years after he detached from the Lewis and Clark Expedition and began a new life as the first of a new generation of fur trappers and mountain men. Rather than a faithful rendering of the man's appearance, this image perhaps better illustrates the popular myth that grew up around this larger-than-life figure. The image is light on facts; rather than the dates given, Colter was born some time between 1770 and 1775 and died in 1812 or 1813. (Courtesy of the Wyoming State Archives.)

This photograph shows the men and pack stock of the Hayden Expedition making their way over the rough Wyoming ranges in a day and age before established trails or roads. The expedition passed through the Jackson region on its way to what would soon become Yellowstone National Park in an effort to increase Euro-Americans' scientific understanding of the region and its flora, fauna, geology, and human societies. An undertaking like this required thousands of pounds of gear, including basic supplies but also highly complex and fragile observational equipment, transported on stock over rough terrain. (Courtesy of the Wyoming State Archives.)

Ferdinand Vandeever Hayden was born in Massachusetts in 1829 and studied geology and medicine before serving the Union army in the Civil War as a doctor. But he is best known for the series of western expeditions that he led in the 12 years following the end of the Civil War. His 1871 exploration of Yellowstone, pictured here, was instrumental in the decision the following year to designate the region as the world's first national park. (Courtesy of the Wyoming State Archives.)

This photograph, also from the 1871 Hayden Expedition, shows the team camped in Teton Canyon on the other side of the range from Jackson Hole. A young moose and other fresh game hang from a wooden rack, while a hungry-looking man with a hatchet gets ready for some butchering. The constant work of traveling, hunting for meat, and making scientific observations no doubt would have left snippets of free time like this as a precious refuge. (Courtesy of the Wyoming State Archives.)

A modern, 19th-century scientific expedition needed a variety of skill sets and specialties in order to collect the kind of information that the team's backers wanted. Some of these experts are tagged on the bottom of the photograph by Jackson, including W.R. Taggart, who served as assistant geologist. E. Campbell Carrington served as zoologist, while William Henry Holmes was the artist and illustrator who replaced Thomas Moran. (Courtesy of the American Heritage Center, University of Wyoming.)

16

Pictured is Richard "Beaver Dick" Leigh and his family. Leigh was a trapper who settled in the valley when the Rocky Mountain fur trade ended as a viable career, turning instead to a combination of hunting, trapping, guiding, and ranching. He guided the Hayden Expedition when it visited in the 1870s. From left to right are Beaver Dick, John, Anne Jane, Jenny with an unidentified child in her lap, and William on the mule. It was very common in the days of the fur trade for Euro-American trappers to marry Native women. This provided companionship for the long years in the mountains but also plugged them into Indigenous social and trade networks, including a vast array of regionally specific knowledge. Jenny's name is preserved in today's landscape through her inspiration for the name of Jenny Lake. (Courtesy of the American Heritage Center, University of Wyoming.)

Beaver Dick is pictured here with his second family. In 1876, after caring for a woman with smallpox, his entire family became sick and passed away. In the Wyoming of the 19th century, far from definitive care, disease destroyed many families like Beaver Dick's. On the left side of this photograph is Susan Tadpole, the Bannock woman he married after the disaster, and the three children they raised, William, Rose, and Emma. (Courtesy of the American Heritage Center, University of Wyoming.)

This camp scene from the final days of the Hayden Expedition shows a mix of Indigenous and Euro-American symbols: a Native man with both a gun and bow, the American flag and an animal hide hanging side by side on the wooden pole, and the white man sitting in front of the teepee. The stated goal of the expedition was to learn about the region's physical environment, but the effort was intertwined with, and reliant on, the Native people that called these ranges home. (Courtesy of the American Heritage Center, University of Wyoming.)

This photograph is from the extended 1883 trip of Pres. Chester A. Arthur, Secretary of War Robert Lincoln, and Lt. Gen. Philip Sheridan to Jackson Hole and the Yellowstone Country. After Arthur succeeded to the presidency upon the death of James Garfield, he was plagued by a chronic kidney disease. This trip was part of an effort to shake off rumors of his poor health during his unsuccessful bid to secure the Republican nomination the following year. The route that the party took into Jackson Hole became known as the "Bottle Trail" thanks to the volume of bottles the heavy-drinking men discarded from the saddle. The presidential trip foreshadowed a generation of rich hunters who would travel to Wyoming from the East for long hunting trips. (Courtesy of the Wyoming State Archives.)

Two

LIFE IN EARLY JACKSON

As the 20th century dawned in Jackson, it was a busy albeit isolated and small frontier town. The passage of state game laws after the granting of statehood in 1890 allowed for the development of a nascent elk hunting industry, a seasonal pursuit that supported 25 out of the 75 families living in the valley. The promise of this industry for a region that had never been economically dynamic was a prime factor in the run-up to the Indian War of 1895. Despite these conflicts, the town remained a place where Euro-Americans and Native people lived side by side.

Jackson's rows of streets and lots were laid out in 1901 along a plat designed by Grace Miller on land that she owned with her husband, Robert. This first plat encompassed the area today bounded by Deloney Street on the south, Flat Creek to the north and west, and Cache Street on the east. The Millers had been in Jackson for a while; Robert became the first man to bring wagons over the pass in 1885. He dug irrigation ditches and managed the largest herd of cattle in the valley before returning to Illinois to marry Grace in 1893. Before the turn of the century, the Millers grazed a cattle herd as large as 500 head at a point in Jackson history when the average herd size was in the 30s.

Lots in the new town were sold, and the young community was incorporated in 1911. The intersection of Deloney and Cache Streets grew into the nucleus of the town, with Charles Deloney's store, a livery stable, a saloon, and the Jackson Hotel all sitting near that intersection. Census data charts the town's steady rise: 60 residents in 1890 had multiplied into 638 ten years later, and Jackson was home to about 1,500 people by 1910. In these early years, it was not a given that the town of Jackson would emerge as the urban center and logistical hub for the valley; of the 18 post offices opened in Jackson Hole, only six remain today.

Early Jackson lacked the creature comforts and basic necessities familiar to most people of the period. The town's first resident doctor did not arrive until 1916. There was no dentist for the first few decades of town living, but in their stead, the local blacksmith came up with a technique and tools for pulling teeth.

The first sign that Jackson would become a recreation destination predated the town with the controversy over who was the first Euro-American to climb the Grand Teton. James Stevenson and Nathaniel Langford, both members of the 1872 Hayden Expedition, became the first to claim they had made it to the summit, with support from 14 of their survey compatriots. In 1898, William Owen and three companions reached the summit, returning to challenge the earlier climbers' claim: they found no marker (the construction of which was customary upon a first ascent), and the summit was not at all as they described, with craggy blocks of rock instead of the flowers and tracks of mountain sheep that Stevenson and Langford reported.

A local landmark was born when Jackson's Clubhouse was put under construction in 1897. The first resident business in a long line of local commerce was the Jackson Mercantile, which was a mercantile in the Western mold of being able to supply nearly everything a frontier family could need and could usually extend credit until the sale of some cattle provided enough free cash flow to pay the bill. The Jackson Hole Gun Club, the organization chartered to increase the civic life in the young town and build the Clubhouse, changed its name in 1905 to the Jackson Hole Commercial Club, which demonstrates the earnest desire among many town founders to build the community both socially and economically. The Clubhouse became the center of the town, with school held during the day and dances, balls, and concerts held at night.

Change came to Jackson as the 1920s ushered in a new age of consumerism, private car ownership, and regional tourism. The town got its first gas station in 1922 in order to cater to the growing number of tourists making automobile journeys from out of state. These drivers benefited from a frenzy of road building in the 1920s, followed by New Deal programs in the 1930s that built roadside picnic areas, hiking trails, roads, and other tourist-friendly infrastructure on public lands, especially around national parks. The town got a high-profile visit in 1926 when the crown prince and princess of Sweden spent some time on their way to see Yellowstone and the Tetons.

These two photographs are from Owen Wister's 1887 trip to Jackson, the first a formal studio shoot in town and the second from his group's hunting expedition (with Wister posing pouring something from a bottle into his friend's cup). Wister was a friend of Theodore Roosevelt, which likely contributed to his desire for a big Western hunting trip. His writing career had just started to take off, and it blossomed after the 1902 publication of *The Virginian*, but his several trips to Wyoming in the 1880s and 1890s provided the material for the man who is today regarded as the father of the Western novel. Yet Wister brought his Eastern sensibilities and prejudices, resulting in work that depicted a mythologized Old West, a process that continues today. (Both, Owen Wister Papers, courtesy of the American Heritage Center, University of Wyoming.)

Albert Nelson, a Swedish immigrant, found Wyoming through work in the 1880s on the railroad. After a career of mine prospecting, hunting, ranching, taxidermy, and general mountain living, he became Wyoming's first game warden. After serving three years he resigned, wearied by the unpopular game laws, meager pay, and difficult conditions and eager to get back to his homestead. This photograph shows Nelson's forest camp in 1899. (J.E. Stimson Collection, courtesy of the Wyoming State Archives.)

This 1901 photograph shows Allen's Hotel, located near the outlet of Jackson Lake. Four men sit outside shooting the breeze. This landscape would be dramatically refashioned with the construction of Jackson Dam beginning 10 years later. The photograph was taken by Joseph Elam Stimson, an early photographer in Jackson Hole. (J.E. Stimson Collection, courtesy of the Wyoming State Archives.)

Early-20th-century Jackson is shown here as a thriving small town. Multiple two-story buildings in the core of the village show its success over other would-be towns in Jackson Hole. By this time, there would have been a trickle of hunters and tourists moving through the town, foreshadowing much larger waves who would come after the Tetons were established as a national park. Jackson became the place to stop on the way to the mountains to get supplies and one last hot meal before the trials of the wilderness. (Courtesy of the Wyoming State Archives.)

Jackson's Clubhouse became the center of community life after it was built in 1897. This photograph shows a group that was gathered there for a dance in 1903. The role of the Clubhouse, or that of dances like this, cannot be overstated, tying together a disparate and remote valley into a coherent community. With homesteads and ranches placed far apart, gatherings like this would have given people of all ages an opportunity to meet and socialize. (S.N. Leek Papers, courtesy of the American Heritage Center, University of Wyoming.)

Grace and Robert Miller are pictured here on horseback in front of their cabin. This couple was intimately involved with the development of Jackson, with Grace platting out the first town lots on land they owned at the core of today's town and later serving as one of the first mayors. Robert served in a variety of land management roles, helping to steward the valley's natural resources and forest lands. This ranch would later become a core piece of the National Elk Refuge. (Courtesy of the Wyoming State Archives.)

This 1920 shot of the two-story log Episcopal Hospital shows the facilities that Jacksonites in need would have relied on. The first substantive hospital in town, it was built in 1916 with the support of St. John's Episcopal Church. The presence or lack of a hospital could spell survival or doom for a small Western town on the margin of boom and bust economic cycles. (Courtesy of the Wyoming State Archives.)

This photograph shows the first all-woman town government in Jackson, elected in 1920. From left to right are (first row) town council member Rose Crabtree, Mayor Grace Miller, and town council member Fausting Haight; (second row) town council members Genevieve Van Vleck and Mae Deloney. The administration was a success, with an ordinance prohibiting loose livestock in city limits, the construction of a road to and purchase of land from the US Forest Service for a cemetery, and the signing of a contract with Edward Benson to provide electric power to the town, though this project would take several years. Grace Miller, along with her husband, Robert, owned the land on which the town was originally platted, with Grace doing much of the surveying herself. Robert served as forest supervisor for Teton National Forest between 1908 and 1918, selling much of their land to the nascent National Elk Refuge. (Courtesy of the Wyoming State Archives.)

Despite some success and development in the 1920s, early Jackson remained a rudimentary place. This 1928 photograph of Charles Brown's dentist's chair, located in his home, depicts the extent of dental care available in town. In a day and age when disease and mortality were much higher than today, a practicing dentist, however rudimentary his facilities might be, was a godsend for Jackson. (Courtesy of the Wyoming State Archives.)

Fraternal organizations such as the Freemasons played a large role in Jackson, as they did across the American West. Here, men could socialize with their neighbors and talk politics, business, or gossip. This 1929 photograph shows the US Forest Service warehouse where Jackson's leading men met to apply to the Grand Lodge of Wyoming for a Jackson lodge. The request was granted, and later that summer, Jackson Lodge No. 48 AFAM opened its doors. (Frank J. Meyers Papers, courtesy of the American Heritage Center, University of Wyoming.)

This shot of Jackson's main square in 1930 shows the front exteriors of the Jackson Drug Company, Jackson Mercantile, and hardware store. In the background is Snow King, which in 1930 would have been called Town Hill and would have sported only a small ski jump, built in 1926 by Mike O'Neil. Two years later, the hill would be renamed Ruth Hanna Simms Ski Hill in honor of a local woman who donated the money to develop skiing on the hill, and six years later, the Civilian Conservation Corps built a horseback riding and hiking trail to the summit. (Courtesy of the Wyoming State Archives.)

This is a 1931 photograph of Fred Lovejoy's Log Cabin Café. As the owner and operator of the Jackson Telephone Company, Lovejoy was one of the first residents of Jackson to have telephone service. The café was a business venture designed to cater to the growing cascade of travelers who wanted to see the brand-new Grand Teton National Park. (Courtesy of the American Heritage Center, University of Wyoming.)

This photograph from 1933 shows men planting trees in Jackson's Town Square in front of the Jackson Mercantile. A man in the foreground seems to be holding the traces of a team of stock, contrasting with the cars parked behind him in a typical Western fashion. The Great Depression would have been tough for communities like Jackson and businesses like the mercantile, but the economy's isolation from the wider world insulated it from the vagaries of unbridled capitalism. Make-work projects of the New Deal also put money in people's pockets and led to the development of new facilities on public lands. (Courtesy of the American Heritage Center, University of Wyoming.)

Jackson, Wyo - 1936.

RINK.

RUTH HANNA SIMM SKI HILL.

This 1936 aerial view of town shows some development since the turn of the century, but it still depicts a sleepy mountain town. An arrow points out the skating rink, and lettering labels the Ruth Hanna Simms Ski Hill. The four years following this scene would see much development. In 1937, the Jackson Hole Ski Association would be organized, with the town purchasing seven acres at the base of the hill in 1939 and installing the Old Man's Flats rope tow, the first lift on the recently renamed Snow King Mountain. (Courtesy of the Wyoming State Archives.)

Jackson Grade School's class of 1939 is pictured here, with all dressed up in their fanciest clothes. The arrival and expansion of a school in a frontier town like Jackson would have meant a lot to early residents, representing a certain status for the town and a certain level of opportunity for its young people. (Courtesy of the Wyoming State Archives.)

This undated photograph depicts a sight familiar in Jackson: snow-covered streets and sidewalks. It also shows the front exterior of Jackson Hole Toggery, Square Deal Grocer, and the hardware store. Removing snow and keeping the town functioning during the long Wyoming winter is a monumental task. (Courtesy of the Wyoming State Archives.)

This photograph, taken from the slopes of Snow King, shows a growing town nestled beneath the Gros Ventre Buttes. By the 1920s, Jackson had established itself as the central town of the valley. It was a community in flux, transitioning away from its roots as a remote ranching economy into one catering to an increasing flow of visitors headed to new national parks. (Courtesy of the Wyoming State Archives.)

This photograph shows Jackson's Pure Food Club. Clubs such as these were part of a broad Progressive Era social movement that aimed for stricter food safety laws and fought against corporations that mislabeled food or included dangerous nonfood ingredients in their products. The movement won a signal victory in 1906 when the Pure Food and Drug Act created the Food and Drug Administration and empowered the US Bureau of Chemistry to inspect food products, though it would take more consumer protection laws and a few decades before producers would be held to higher standards of food purity. (S.N. Leek Papers, courtesy of the American Heritage Center, University of Wyoming.)

Avalanche paths blend into ski runs on the slopes of Mount Snow King as the town of Jackson sits beneath, free of snow. This early-20th-century photograph shows a town that had outgrown its sleepy cattle ranching days and established itself as the commercial hub of northwestern Wyoming. (S.N. Leek Papers, courtesy of the American Heritage Center, University of Wyoming.)

Jackson's two-story Public School House was a testament to the town's growth. In this shot, the stacks of chopped firewood beneath denuded slopes are also testament to the ecological impacts of the town's expansion. (S.N. Leek Papers, courtesy of the American Heritage Center, University of Wyoming.)

Bundled Jacksonites brave the cold to attend the formal opening of this bridge over the Snake River. A dog waits patiently for his turn to cross. The river had long defined mobility networks within the valley, proving fatal to some of the first Euro-American explorations. (S.N. Leek Papers, courtesy of the American Heritage Center, University of Wyoming.)

Stephen Leek sits on a barrel perched in a wagon in front of his ranch house. The melting snow suggests the transitions between seasons that would have governed life in early-20th-century Jackson. (S.N. Leek Papers, courtesy of the American Heritage Center, University of Wyoming.)

Two local boys cling to the back of a patient burro. Relationships with animals—both imported farmyard animals and their wild neighbors—started at a young age would have added a richness to life in rural Wyoming. (S.N. Leek Papers, courtesy of the American Heritage Center, University of Wyoming.)

This photograph by Stephen Leek in the 1900s or 1910s shows a nascent town poised for growth. A few two-story buildings can be seen at the center of town, including the Clubhouse and a few hotels, but at this early stage, Jackson remained a dispersed, small-scale settlement. Leek's conservation efforts, especially his photographs of Jackson Hole's elk, resulted in increased visibility and protection of the valley's natural resources. (S.N. Leek Papers, courtesy of the American Heritage Center, University of Wyoming.)

OPPOSITE: Three children attempt to have some fun with a broken cart. Growing up on a rural Jackson Hole ranch would have been an isolating experience at times, but the simple living and natural environment could also have been an imaginative child's paradise. (S.N. Leek Papers, courtesy of the American Heritage Center, University of Wyoming.)

This panorama by Stephen Leek shows the small hamlet of Jackson developing beside Flat Creek. From its earliest days, terrain and the elements have governed life in Jackson, with winter roaring in and frustrating human ambition. Those who have survived have done so by preparing year-

round and accepting the dictates of the environment. (S.N. Leek Papers, courtesy of the American Heritage Center, University of Wyoming.)

These panoramic shots, taken by Stephen Leek between 1890 and 1940, show the town of Jackson growing over time as it slips the robes of winter on and off. (Both, S.N. Leek Papers, courtesy of

the American Heritage Center, University of Wyoming.)

The O.P. Skaggs Store, pictured in this photograph, was a place where Jackson residents could go for all manner of groceries and fresh foods. Early grocery stores like this would cater to locals but also the increasing flow of tourists passing through Jackson on their way to the Tetons and Yellowstone. (S.N. Leek Papers, courtesy of the American Heritage Center, University of Wyoming.)

A little boy is pictured on the Leek Ranch outside of Jackson with a mountain lion that was killed. Bounties paid for the killing of predators dramatically changed the speciation profile of the American West, and Jackson Hole is no exception. Coyotes, bears, mountain lions, and other species were slaughtered by settlers, usually with prompting by the livestock industry and ranchers. Federal and state government programs focused on killing predators continue to this day. (S.N. Leek Papers, courtesy of the American Heritage Center, University of Wyoming.)

Jackson Hole's boys' baseball team is seen here posing in front of the park's stands, probably some time in the 1930s. Recreational opportunities like this helped to knit the town and region together and signaled the end of Jackson's frontier stage. (S.N. Leek Papers, courtesy of the American Heritage Center, University of Wyoming.)

Early automobiles, some of the first seen in the broad-bottomed Jackson Hole, are parked outside the Stringer Hotel. A saddled horse stands nearby, perhaps wondering if he will soon be relieved of his person-carrying duties by more of the new machines. More private automobiles began arriving in Jackson in the 1930s, and hoteliers like the Stringers catered to this clientele. (Hugo G. Janssen Photographs, courtesy of the American Heritage Center, University of Wyoming.)

A man named Moyer and his sister stand next to an early fan-driven snowmobile. Since the early days of Euro-American settlement, the mobility challenges of the terrain, especially in winter, limited development. But as the 20th century progressed, new technology offered a potential amelioration of some of these challenges. Innovation like this would also lead to new forms of recreational technology, with snowmobiling today comprising a sizeable portion of winter recreation. (Frank J. Meyers Papers, courtesy of the American Heritage Center, University of Wyoming.)

Pictured is the family of Albert Nelson, who in the 1890s served as Wyoming's first game warden. He became an active community member and was behind the construction of the Clubhouse and other social events around Jackson. In his lifetime, he advanced from a hard-working immigrant without prospects to a man of considerable property and social clout in Jackson. He worked in his taxidermy shop nearly until the day that he died in 1957 at the age of 95. (J.E. Stimson Collection, courtesy of the Wyoming State Archives.)

A motorized saw like this would have been revolutionary in a town like Jackson. The constant drudgery of sawing and chopping wood in order to keep cabins and houses warm through the long Wyoming winter would have been improved by this device, which could quickly cut long logs into sections to be split. The manual saw that this device would have replaced is leaning against the porch railing. (S.N. Leek Papers, courtesy of the American Heritage Center, University of Wyoming.)

This photograph, from the 1940s or 1950s, shows three men sitting in a corral with their rifles. While weapons like these would have been standard tools of the trade for people who needed to hunt and trap to feed their families, it is also a testament to the enduring place of violence in the American West. A society founded on the dispossession of Native land remains a violent place, with more than its fair share of toxic masculinity. (S.N. Leek Papers, courtesy of the American Heritage Center, University of Wyoming.)

This 1964 photograph features James Mangus leaning against an old car. Mangus, "Jimmy" to his friends and neighbors, was an old Jackson Hole pioneer who never left the area. In his later years, Mangus was living on a homestead near the base of the Grand Teton to the south of Jenny Lake with his elderly mother. Old-timers like Mangus have a way of sticking around Jackson. (David F. Delap Papers, courtesy of the American Heritage Center, University of Wyoming.)

Three

INTERACTIONS WITH NATURE

When Euro-American settlers trekked into the heart of the North American continent, the most important technology they brought with them was a barnyard menagerie of domesticated animals. These herds were ungulates like cattle and sheep and horses alongside smaller numbers of swine, fowl, and goats. They were driven before the settlers, and it would be on their backs that a new economy would be built. The efforts of fur trappers, gold prospectors, and government explorers made the first several years of Euro-American history around Jackson a story of itinerants. When the first generation came to stay in the 1870s, 1880s, and 1890s, they chose ranching as the basis of their society and economy. There were early attempts at farming, and some success, but the harsh weather of the region would always make it difficult for agriculture. Thus the grasses of the valley became the foundation upon which a ranching economy was built.

Ranching would add much to early Jackson's economy, but perhaps its biggest contribution would be to American culture with the mythic image of the cowboy keeping watch over his herd against the challenges of the open range. Ranch life was different in Jackson Hole; here were not the massive herds of sprawling estates and long-distance drives of Texas but more small-scale family businesses. Each family had to work to grow and lay in a supply of hay that would get the animals through the punishing winter, or they would have to move their herds out of the Hole and down into greener winter pastures. These conditions kept herds small and operations simple, with one estimate putting the total number of cattle in the valley in 1900 at less than 1,000. There was not much money in it, but it was better than farming.

As the ranching economy grew in scale and diversified, conflict broke out between those who ranged cattle and those managing large herds of sheep. This conflict was repeated in every range across the West, but in Jackson Hole, it saw three spasms of violence between the two camps in 1896, 1898, and 1901.

This all changed when Jackson Hole was discovered as a vacation destination. The trend among the wealthy in the late 1800s began to shift from African safaris to hunting trips in the American West, thanks in part to the high-profile travels of Theodore Roosevelt. Jackson ranchers jumped on this trend, with most choosing to guide hunters at least part-time. In 1883, Jackson Hole got a high-profile visit from Pres. Chester A. Arthur, who traveled with Secretary of War Robert Lincoln, Lt. Gen. Philip Sheridan, and a huge cohort of assistants and guides. The party drank so much that the route they used to access the valley became known as the Bottle Trail thanks to the regular markers of castaway bottles from the presidential party.

But above all other species, the pride of Jackson Hole has always been its elk herds, the largest in North America. The arrival of the first generation of market hunters in the late 1890s and their voluminous success in gunning down the big targets suggested to many the need for some kind of protection. The hunters killed the 500- to 700-pound animals principally for their tusks, as their small canine teeth are called. They were used for jewelry and were particularly popular with members of the Order of Elks. A 1901 letter to Pres. Theodore Roosevelt has A.A. Anderson, a supervisor for the newly created forest reserve, nearly begging for more resources to combat the tuskers. "Until my present [inspection] trip . . . I had no idea of the number of elk being slaughtered," he explained to the conservation-minded president. "No portion of the carcasses had been touched except [for] the removal of the tusks."

The establishment of the Teton Game Preserve in 1905 was a step in the right direction but not far enough. The winter of 1909 saw a large die-off of at least half of the entire herd. Jackson ranchers tried to help out with some supplemental feeding, but it was always the case that the elks' need was highest when the ranchers' own cattle herds were also in the toughest position. Before the winter was over, the Wyoming legislature came through with $5,000 for the purchase of hay, with Congress following in 1911 with an additional $20,000 appropriation.

The elks regained the semblance of a home with the 1912 establishment of the National Elk Refuge. The federal government bought 2,000 acres of private meadows, joined it to thousands of acres of public land, and used this as the nucleus for further purchases. The Izaak Walton League bought 2,000 acres adjoining the refuge and donated it. This preservation can be principally attributed to the efforts of Stephen N. Leek. Leek's photographs, many of which are included in this chapter, moved hearts and minds on the Eastern speakers' circuit.

Scientists studying Jackson's elks have used the herds to broaden their understanding of their biology and ecology. The long residency of Olaus and Margaret Murie demonstrates this, with the former publishing the seminal *The Elk of North America* and discovering necrotic stomatitis, a disease that leads to the breakdown of mucous membranes in the mouth, while working in Jackson Hole. After a long and effective career, Margaret Murie was called the "Grandmother of the Conservation Movement" by the Sierra Club and Wilderness Society.

These workers, depicted on the job in 1910, are using a crane to stack hay rather than the more common tip-up. Stacking the hay increased its longevity, which was important considering how, in climates with winters as cold as Jackson, supplemental feed could often mean the difference between livestock making it through the winter and suffering heavy losses to one's herd. Note the horse-drawn wagon in the foreground. (Courtesy of the Wyoming State Archives.)

Four men work hard to stack hay, their frenetic labors blurring their form in this early photograph. A fifth man watching from a seat must have really just needed a second to catch his breath. The bundled men and snowy landscape suggest this is a midwinter scene, the part of the winter where ranches turn to hay cached during warmer months. (S.N. Leek Papers, courtesy of the American Heritage Center, University of Wyoming.)

This photograph is from the Leek Ranch, south of town, in the 1910s or 1920s. The man and horses are working together to build a haystack, a partnership that made settlement of Jackson, and many places like it, possible. Human societies in the 19th- and 20th-century American West were built on the backs of pack stock. (S.N. Leek Papers, courtesy of the American Heritage Center, University of Wyoming.)

This photograph, also from the Leek Ranch, shows an unusual barnyard combination—horses, cows, and elks exist side by side as they all attempt to survive the harsh Jackson winter. Normally flighty around people or domesticated livestock, hungry elks were made docile by their desperation. (S.N. Leek Papers, courtesy of the American Heritage Center, University of Wyoming.)

A local man named Pap Carter is pictured here in his treasured wheat field. Early settlers in the valley were forced to choose between farming and ranching, with most finding the former too difficult given the short growing season and harsh conditions. While many had a small garden plot and a hay field for winter livestock feed, others, like Carter, found a measure of success in farming (S.N. Leek Papers, courtesy of the American Heritage Center, University of Wyoming.)

These two men, pictured in the 1910s or 1920s, are admiring the potatoes growing on the Leek Ranch. While farming got a slower start around Jackson compared to ranching, Jacksonites eventually found the crops, methods, and terrain that worked well for growing food. (S.N. Leek Papers, courtesy of the American Heritage Center, University of Wyoming.)

Hay was the most widely grown crop in early Jackson by far. After harvesting, it would be gathered and stacked in order to provide supplemental feed, the make-or-break holdover fed to animals when deep winter snows covered over the browse and put survival into question. (S.N. Leek Papers, courtesy of the American Heritage Center, University of Wyoming.)

This 1944 photograph is from Battle Mountain Ranch, which was experimenting with dryland farming techniques. These techniques, discredited by the Dust Bowl of the 1920s and susceptible to changes in precipitation patterns, survived in arid places like Jackson. Pictured are owners Dr. Lladd Lacey and Wallace Haittee, who claimed that this unirrigated field produced 50 bushels of barley per acre. (Courtesy of the Wyoming State Archives.)

This 1957 photograph shows Spring Creek Valley, to the west of Jackson. The creek flows parallel with and between the Snake River and Flat Creek, meandering through rich pasture and feeding springtime blooms of wildflowers. The photograph was taken by Finis Mitchell, a prominent conservationist of Wyoming landscapes. (Finis Mitchell Papers, courtesy of the American Heritage Center, University of Wyoming.)

This photograph was taken in 1957 on Big Ranch, which was located near Spring Creek. Perhaps there is no more stereotypically Western image than a young man sitting on a split-rail fence and staring off wistfully into the distance while wildflowers bloom at his feet and snowy ranges tower above him. (Finis Mitchell Papers, courtesy of the American Heritage Center, University of Wyoming.)

This picture shows Wyoming governor B.B. Brooks (second from left) and game warden D.C. Nowlin alongside three other men, all bundled warmly in the back of a sled. Visible in the background are two druggists' shops, an essential feature of any Western settlement. The men were likely headed out of town to view the elk herds. Brooks was governor from 1905 until 1911 and got his start as a cowboy trailing cattle from the Snake River to the plains of central Wyoming before transitioning from beaver trapper to rancher along the Big Muddy River. In 2018, Brooks was named to the Wyoming Cowboy Hall of Fame. (Courtesy of the Wyoming State Archives.)

This hunter stands over an elk he shot somewhere along Harris Creek, above the floor of Jackson Hole. Jackson's elk herds were hunted throughout the 20th century by locals looking to put meat on their table, market hunters looking only to harvest and sell their teeth, and easterners on big game hunting safaris. (Courtesy of the Wyoming State Archives.)

People came to the National Elk Refuge for more than just hunting—it was a curiosity to many. The proximity of the National Elk Refuge, founded in 1912 and expanding quickly thereafter, made it a popular place for a bit of silly fun. This shot from the 1910s or 1920s shows a man tempting a hungry elk with a treat in his mouth. (Courtesy of the Wyoming State Archives.)

Jackson Hole has long been home to North America's largest elk herds. But as the 20th century dawned, they were facing new challenges of intense market hunting (aimed only at their incisor teeth, which were used for jewelry) and habitat loss. Action only began after the winter of 1909, when harsh conditions and pasture loss led to the death of half the herd. Ranchers helped where they could with supplemental feeding, but they were stretched to the limit themselves. The state legislature appropriated $5,000 for the purchase of hay, and Congress followed two years later with $20,000. These early stopgap measures would evolve into efforts to protect elk habitat, resulting in the National Elk Refuge familiar today. The photograph above shows a horse-drawn wagon on runners being used to distribute hay, and below, Holly Leek, Stephen Leek's youngest son, hand-feeds elk near his family's ranch. (Both, S.N. Leek Papers, courtesy of the American Heritage Center, University of Wyoming.)

This photograph from the 1910s or 1920s begins to hint at the scale of Jackson Hole's elk herds. The flat bottom of the valley provides a refuge when winter blows into the mountains, though, as this photograph demonstrates, winter also makes itself felt in the valley, which can frustrate the elks' grazing. (S.N. Leek Papers, courtesy of the American Heritage Center, University of Wyoming.)

A man stands next to a young elk who is the lone survivor of a group desperate to get to the hay protected by this wooden stockade. Ranchers stored supplemental feed for their own domesticated herds and spared what they could for the elks. (S.N. Leek Papers, courtesy of the American Heritage Center, University of Wyoming.)

This photograph from April 1914 shows two bull elks sparring. Males lock antlers and push each other around to determine hierarchy and mating opportunities, especially during the wintertime rut. Some of the other males look on the brawl with interest, but the rest of the herd seems nonplussed. (Courtesy of the Wyoming State Archives.)

Neither party blinks as this man on skis gestures at a bull elk in Jackson Hole. Interactions between the valley's elk herds and more recent human occupants have been a constant part of life here. Note the single long stave, which earlier skiers would have used to propel themselves by pushing between their legs. (Courtesy of the Marriott Digital Library, University of Utah.)

This photograph from the early 1920s shows the same man and bull elk sizing each other up from a distance. (Courtesy of the Marriott Digital Library, University of Utah.)

A surprised elk is photographed as he munches on a haystack. It is unclear if he got around the fence seen behind him or if this pile was intentionally left for the herds. Supplemental feeding in the depths of winter made the difference between survival and large-scale die-offs. (Courtesy of the Marriott Digital Library, University of Utah.)

Elk antlers are the subject of much scrutiny in this campfire scene. Around the fire, Jacksonites can relive and retell stories about hunts from earlier that day or from long ago. The youth and giddiness of the boy at the center of the photograph suggests this is one of his first such campfire hangs. (S.N. Leek Papers, courtesy of the American Heritage Center, University of Wyoming.)

Stephen Leek lounges in the warm light of the campfire with a distant look in his eye, seemingly unaware of the mirthful story or teasing being shared around the table behind him. Well-used pans and kettles in front of the fire suggest a bountiful dinner. (S.N. Leek Papers, courtesy of the American Heritage Center, University of Wyoming.)

A group of women, men, and children enjoys a breakfast in camp. The rear of a chuck wagon with a camp tender hard at work can just barely be seen on the right side. The stools, attire, and mixed-gender group all suggest an upper-class pleasure trip. (S.N. Leek Papers, courtesy of the American Heritage Center, University of Wyoming.)

Stephen Leek is pictured on the right alongside a group of men busily disemboweling a dead elk. The clumps of hay and feeding elks behind the men are the results of a winter feeding program begun in the 1910s. (S.N. Leek Papers, courtesy of the American Heritage Center, University of Wyoming.)

A band of elks is seen in this photograph from the 1920s or 1930s advancing toward the town of Jackson. The bare slopes of Snow King behind the town afford a sense of scale. No doubt the resources of town would have been a tempting target for starving herds. (Courtesy of the Wyoming State Archives.)

Stephen Leek arrived in the valley at the age of 30 and established a ranch about three miles south of today's Jackson. As a witness to the elk die-offs of the 1900s and 1910s, he launched himself into advocating for the herd, mainly through photography and public speaking on their behalf. His legacy is complicated, having participated in the murderous Indian War of 1895, but today he is remembered as the "Father of the Elk." (Courtesy of the Wyoming State Archives.)

Leek continued to photograph the valley and its ungulate inhabitants. Like many, he made a living by stitching together a variety of activities—trapping, raising cattle, hosting tourists, and guiding hunters—all united by the through line of close observation of the natural world. Both in these efforts and in his photography, he set the template for a successful Jackson Hole settler. He lived in Jackson Hole from 1888 until his death in 1941. (S.N. Leek Papers, courtesy of the American Heritage Center, University of Wyoming.)

This photograph, taken in the 1940s or 1950s from the rolling benchlands above the valley floor, represents a coalescence of a Western mentality: a trigger-happy Euro-American with multiple weapons on horseback, ostensibly hunting but also projecting a violence toward and distrust of outsiders. (Courtesy of the Wyoming State Archives.)

A group of three hunters proudly displays the fruits of their hunt: geese, ducks, and pheasants. The fine dress, watch, and embroidered gun case suggest men of some means, probably out-of-towners from Eastern cities. By the time this photograph was taken in the 1940s or 1950s, this would have been a very typical Jackson experience, with more and more hunters arriving each season. (Courtesy of the Wyoming State Archives.)

This wagon is well-suited to Teton Pass, having swapped its wheels for snow runners. From the early days of Jackson to today, the terrain and climate have limited mobility. Most early traffic went over Teton Pass or approached Jackson from the south up the Snake River Canyon. Today, Highway 22 connects Jackson to Idaho via Teton Pass. (Courtesy of the Wyoming State Archives.)

Once cars became the primary mode of transportation and roads became ubiquitous, the winter chore above all became keeping those roads clear of snow. Here, a rotary plow works the county road that connects Jackson to Kelly, with two men and a boy watching from the high snowbank. (Courtesy of the Wyoming State Archives.)

A solitary silhouette provides relief and scale in this image from 1949 as plows and road workers struggle to keep the road clear after an inundation of snow. Jackson's elevation, latitude, and topography have always made it a place subjected to the full brunt of the elements. The same forces that make the valley a skier's dream also make it a plow operator's nightmare. (Courtesy of the Wyoming State Archives.)

This aerial shot shows the aftermath of the January 1969 Crater Lake Slide, which buried Highway 22 between Jackson and Teton Pass. The road up to Teton Pass crosses multiple avalanche slide paths, making this a constant worry of travelers attempting to get over the mountains in winter. (Courtesy of the Wyoming State Archives.)

Three men ski into a snowy oblivion surveying the Leek Ranch. Cross-country skiing was the preferred form of winter transportation a full generation or two before downhill skiing arrived in Jackson. The snow-covered slopes of the hills rimming the valley and the mountains beyond suggest the isolation that early Jacksonites must have felt when winter closed the links with the rest of the world. (S.N. Leek Papers, courtesy of the American Heritage Center, University of Wyoming.)

This winter scene snows the Snake River in the foreground and the snow-covered Tetons in the distance. The flat bottom of Jackson Hole makes it a unique haven in a mountainous region. Finis Mitchell took this photograph in 1959. (Finis Mitchell Papers, courtesy of the American Heritage Center, University of Wyoming.)

In the years following the establishment of Grand Teton National Park and its later enlargement, most area ranchers dropped their opposition to the federal presence and came to appreciate the role that tourism could play in the region's economy. Many adopted a mixed business model that combined traditional ranching with hosting tourists interested in trail rides or ranch stays. This 1959 photograph of a ranch house in front of the Grand Teton has fresh laundry hanging in the Wyoming sunshine. (Finis Mitchell Papers, courtesy of the American Heritage Center, University of Wyoming.)

Native people survived the arrival of Euro-American settlers, showing the resilience and indomitable spirit of people even under the worst conditions. But Native people and their cultural symbols were also appropriated and folded into a mythologized story about the West. These teepees, pictured in 1959, were likely located on a dude ranch catering to Euro-American tourists. (Finis Mitchell Papers, courtesy of the American Heritage Center, University of Wyoming.)

Four

RODEO

Rodeo comes from the Spanish word for encircling, a technique used when moving cattle from where they grazed to where they could be sorted, separated, branded, and become more familiar with the sight and scent of humans. With laws passed down from the Spanish viceroy in 1551 and 1571, it is an ancient practice. The rodeo is a scene in the American folk imagination, but initially it was a scene of Spanish-speaking ranchers and Mexican, Native, and Black ranch hands, called vaqueros. It goes back further than that, with bull wrestling in the ancient Olympic games of the Greeks and bull riding and jumping practiced by the ancient Minoans of Crete, but it was 19th-century rodeo events throughout New Spain at fairgrounds, racetracks, and other festival grounds that would evolve into the modern rodeo.

Rodeo entered American culture when the spoils of the Mexican-American War put Mexican lands and Spanish-speaking societies that had long been organized around ranching economies into the American polity. White cowboys adopted the vernacular, look, skills, and friendly competitions of the vaqueros. The master of reimagining the American West, Buffalo Bill, built on ranch-versus-ranch competitions to put on the first modern rodeo in 1882 in North Platte, Nebraska. Women joined the rodeo circuit in the 1890s, but it was not until a Black Texan named Bill Picket joined the ring that it grew in popularity. Picket, performing at the 1904 Cheyenne Frontier Days, reportedly jumped from his horse to a bull's back, bit its upper lip, and wrestled it to the ground. Early photographers such as Ralph Doubleday took pictures at rodeos that were turned into postcards.

In Jackson's early days, the rodeo was less a professional sport and more just a bunch of ranch guys goofing off. The duties of their everyday work life became opportunities to test one's skill and compare it against peers, and friendly competition among mates, such as informal rodeos and stock-tests at the Elbo Ranch, became competitions. As historian Virginia Huidekoper notes, "In 1911 before the town of Jackson was even incorporated there was a forty-acre rodeo ground, complete with covered grandstand, right in the middle of town." This was the home of the well-known and highly respected Jackson Frontier Days rodeo, a mid-summer rodeo festival that attracted competitors and crowds as big as statewide shows like Cheyenne and Pendleton.

Beginning in the 1910s, local committees that set their own eligibility and other rules began to be replaced by promoters who hired officials, standardized the rules, and limited participation by female, Hispanic, Black, and Native people (who, before this, regularly competed and often won). Accelerating these exclusionary trends was the 1929 death of "superstar cowgirl" Bonnie McCarroll during a bronc riding accident at the Pendleton Rodeo. The incident led many American rodeos to drop women's events, and the Rodeo Association of America was formed the same year out of a desire to bring a more standard format and better safety rules.

Before the Second World War, the most popular rodeo events were trick and fancy roping, where the cowboys had to make shapes with their lassos before roping people or animals. These mid-century contests lacked the chutes, gates, and time limits that characterize today's rodeos.

Rather than charging out of a chute with the bull rider on its back, the bull would be blindfolded and snubbed in the center of the arena, where the rider had to simply jump up and hold on. Rides could last several minutes, with some bull-and-rider pairs disappearing from the audience's view.

In the 1920s and 1930s, traveling rodeos were wildly popular all over the eastern United States, Europe, South America, and East Asia; today's rodeos are more often operating as regular festivals in towns across western North America, Brazil, and Australia. Rodeo is quickly gaining popularity in Brazil, with many of the top bull riders traveling from there to the American West for professional competition.

In today's rodeo circuit, a top-flight performer can earn a half-million dollars in a season, with the winner's purse at some rodeos in excess of a million dollars. And when staying on top of a bull four times over a week-long competition could mean $118,000 in prize money, it is not hard to see connections between today's 600 professional bull riders and the rural ranch hand of a previous generation who imagined the rodeo as a way to escape the backbreaking work of the ranch and range.

Today, Jackson's rodeo is still a vibrant tradition, with events held nearly every Wednesday and Saturday from Memorial Day to Labor Day. It is a great rodeo for veterans or those who have never been, with the full suite of events and age groups (this correspondent's favorite event is the mutton busting, when children ride or race young sheep) at the rodeo grounds beneath Mount Snow King.

This photograph shows Stephen Leek; his wife, Etta Wilson; and their son, Lester, at their Outdoor Life exhibit at the Jackson Frontier Days. They are surrounded by elk antlers, a stuffed and mounted bison head, photographs, and other animal products. Leek was a tireless conservationist and friend to Jackson fauna. (S.N. Leek Papers, courtesy of the American Heritage Center, University of Wyoming.)

This photograph, also from the Jackson Frontier Days festival, shows a group of men near the post office. The yearly festival is embraced by many who take advantage of the opportunity to slip into the aesthetic of the Old West. Note the beaver-felt hat of the man standing at the center, a style that has not been in vogue since the 1830s. (S.N. Leek Papers, courtesy of the American Heritage Center, University of Wyoming.)

The Jackson Frontier Park, home to Jackson's rodeo since the early 20th century, is pictured here with packed bleachers in the middle distance and Snow King looming behind. Judges sit in the wooden enclosure across from the bleachers with a good view of whatever event was happening. (S.N. Leek Papers, courtesy of the American Heritage Center, University of Wyoming.)

This photograph shows a bronc rider, a rodeo event where the rider has to stay atop a bucking horse for as long as possible. Next to him is his pickup rider, the guy responsible for rushing in when he falls off to spirit him to safety or for a midair transfer when the rider has ridden for as long as he needs to. (S.N. Leek Papers, courtesy of the American Heritage Center, University of Wyoming.)

The Jackson Frontier Days rodeo is pictured here in the early days, when the enclosure for this bronc rider would have been little more than a ring of mounted and standing men and women. His hat is in his hand and he is still on the horse, so he was still in the running when the photographer snapped this picture. (S.N. Leek Papers, courtesy of the American Heritage Center, University of Wyoming.)

Pickup men angle in from either side, poised to scoop up this bronc buster if he gets bucked off. The blur between the man's woolly chaps is his hat, held in his right hand and swinging wildly behind his back as the horse attempts to rid himself of his burden. (S.N. Leek Papers, courtesy of the American Heritage Center, University of Wyoming.)

Two men are seen here looping their lariats, a short lasso traditionally used for moving stock short distances, such as from one corral to another. A lariat is used in a variety of rodeo events, with the two men here likely doing some fancy roping, an event where the participant has to make a series of shapes with their rope before lassoing a bull. Fancy roping was the most popular rodeo event before World War II but is seen less often today. (S.N. Leek Papers, courtesy of the American Heritage Center, University of Wyoming.)

In this photograph, a cowboy is on horseback making his way around the racetrack at the Jackson rodeo arena. Spectators line the inside of the track for a view of the horse and rider racing by. Note the only woman in the shot, seen behind the rider with her fancy umbrella. (S.N. Leek Papers, courtesy of the American Heritage Center, University of Wyoming.)

This contemporary shot from the team roping event shows how the Jackson rodeo has evolved over the last century. Team roping requires the two participants to work in concert to lasso the calf as quickly as possible, as opposed to the pell-mell, less-organized events of early rodeos. (Author's collection.)

Children crowd onto the rodeo grounds to participate in a relay race. By the 2020s, rodeos had mostly separated into two groups—professional bull-riding circuit where professional athletes compete for large purses or community-oriented, family-friendly rodeos. The Jackson rodeo's stands may be packed with people visiting from afar, but it has maintained its community connection and laid-back vibe. (Author's collection.)

Five

THE ARRIVAL OF THE NATIONAL PARKS AND THE DEVELOPMENT OF A TOURIST HUB

With the establishment of Yellowstone National Park in 1873 as the world's first national park, Jackson found itself with a new identity: an outfitting post and tourism hub for those looking to venture forth into the protected, yet wild, lands to the north. But Yellowstone in the closing decades of the 19th century and early 20th century remained the domain of upper class sportsmen, and Jackson did not see much park traffic until focus turned towards the valley itself.

As early as 1898, there was a push to establish a new park or to include Jackson Hole in Yellowstone National Park, with a letter from the director of the US Geological Survey advocating for its protection. The problem was that by the time the federal government moved to act on this idea, a majority of the area was settled and private land. This led to a decades-long battle between feds and local ranchers over the protection of the Tetons and Jackson Hole, with states' rights proponents and NIMBYs on one side and the federal government and conservationists on the other. The landscape began suffering from the lack of direction; gas stations, hot dog stands, and shabby hotels sprouted up in an ad hoc, unorganized fashion along the base of the Tetons and near Jenny Lake.

The battle lines shifted when a proposal to dam Jenny and Leigh Lakes turned former opponents into conservationists. Struthers Burt, a dude rancher and popular writer who opposed early protection efforts but changed his mind after bearing witness to the damages of unregulated development, put it best when he said, "I am afraid for my own country unless some help is given it—some wise direction. It is too beautiful and now too famous."

But Jackson Hole got its most impactful advocate when John D. Rockefeller Jr. visited the Tetons with his wife. He asked Horace Albright how such shabby, unsightly development had marred the landscape and realized the answer was simply because it was private land. Despite this unsightly development, Rockefeller was struck by the sublime power of the mountains, later describing them as "quite the grandest and most spectacular mountains I have ever seen . . . a picture of ever-changing beauty which is to me beyond compare." After Rockefeller expressed interest in helping, Albright produced a conservative map outlining the most important properties to protect. Rockefeller told him to think bigger and redraw his map with a landscape-wide protection as the end goal. Rockefeller also agreed to keep the purchases secret, creating a dummy corporation to mask his identity and intentions.

Congress passed an organic act establishing Grand Teton National Park in early 1929, using US Forest Service lands to protect just the major peaks and lakes at the foot of the mountains. The controversy over expanding into Jackson Hole dragged on, and by November 1942, Rockefeller was tired enough to write a letter to the secretary of the interior saying he would divest of the properties within a year, whether or not the government would take them for a park. This pushed President Roosevelt to declare a 200,000-acre national monument out of much of Grand Teton National Forest, other federal lands, and Rockefeller's holdings. This made absolutely everyone irate. A protest movement of local ranchers, led by Hollywood actor Wallace Beery, met up to air grievances and drive their cattle across the national monument boundary, convinced they were going to be turned around by federal agents. The men met up for speeches and drinking in town while their wives corralled the cattle for the drive, yet something happened that prompted the wives to start off toward the national monument, requiring the men to jump into cars and speed north lest they miss the big confrontation. But it was a lot of hot air vented over nothing; there were no federal agents at the boundary, as they had already agreed that existing grazing rights would be protected. The march devolved into a group of disappointed, drunk men throwing beer cans over the boundary.

The late 1940s saw several Congressional attempts to disestablish the national monument, but these grassroots efforts were met with a growing conservation movement. A compromise was hammered out: Teton County would be reimbursed for the loss of tax revenues, grazing rights would be honored for the lifetime of the ranchers, and the park would not allow the hunting of elks but would deputize locals each year as temporary park rangers who could control for excess population. A bill incorporating these compromises and finally creating the Grand Teton National Park Americans know today finally passed Congress in 1950. Since then, the park, and Jackson's role in outfitting and supporting it, has only grown as the region has expanded in popularity, visibility, and importance, as the photographs in the next two chapters will attest.

The postwar years saw a growing popularity of the new parks in addition to a new generation of dude ranches that could accommodate the growing numbers of visitors.

Phelps Lake sits at the mouth of Death Canyon in the southern part of Grand Teton National Park. Phelps was one of six glacial lakes at the foot of the peaks that was protected when the first iteration of the national park was declared in 1929. This shot is from July 1927, just before that establishment. (J.E. Stimson Collection, courtesy of the Wyoming State Archives.)

This shot, from the 1929 dedication of Grand Teton National Park, shows W.H. Jackson (right), the Civil War veteran and famed Western photographer of the Hayden Expedition and other western expeditions, alongside D.W. Greenburg (left). Greenburg was an amateur historian of the American West. (W.D. Johnston Papers, courtesy of the American Heritage Center, University of Wyoming.)

The establishment of the first iteration of Grand Teton National Park was not without controversy, and this 1929 dedication scene was never a given. The first park protected the principal peaks of the range and six natural, glacier-fed lakes at their foot. But much more controversy would follow when the federal government and philanthropist John D. Rockefeller Jr. attempted to expand the park into Jackson Hole. (W.D. Johnston Papers, courtesy of the American Heritage Center, University of Wyoming.)

Horace Albright (left), at the time the superintendent of national parks, and Billy Owen (right), a member of the party that made the first Euro-American ascent of the Grand Teton, shake hands near the foot of the peaks. The photograph was taken by Harrison Crandall, who was the first official park photographer and lived in Jackson Hole from the 1920s to the 1960s. (Courtesy of the Wyoming State Archives.)

This shot, from July 29, 1929, shows a fish dinner that was held during the park's first dedication. Visible on the right side facing the camera in the shade of the trees are Horace Albright (behind woman at right on first row) and Sam Woodring (in glasses), the first superintendent of the park. Woodring was removed by Albright in July 1934 after allegations of impropriety. (Courtesy of the Wyoming State Archives.)

Horace Albright delivers a speech during the dedication of Grand Teton National Park. Wyoming governor Frank C. Emerson is seated at the extreme right. Before ascending to the governorship, Emerson was the Wyoming state engineer and a key proponent of the Colorado River Compact. Many of the teens seated beneath Albright seem more interested in the camera than the speech. (Courtesy of the Wyoming State Archives.)

This photograph shows a man entering a "Standard" cabin at Jackson Lake Lodge as a bellhop, bent over, retrieves his baggage. With more and more tourists arriving in their own automobiles, lodges like Jackson Lake Lodge, with their numerous cabins nearby, provided new opportunities for middle-class tourism. (Courtesy of the Wyoming State Archives.)

The woodlands around Jackson have long been used for idyllic rural retreats. But with the establishment of two national parks nearby and a new generation of postwar motor tourists, camps like this expanded their facilities to meet the new demand. (S.N. Leek Papers, courtesy of the American Heritage Center, University of Wyoming.)

This group of dude girls enjoyed a trip to the Turpin Meadows Dude Ranch in the summer of 1932. The 1920s and 1930s saw explosive growth in Jackson Hole of dude ranches that catered to tourists, usually from urban areas on the East Coast, who wanted to spend a week or two reliving the atavistic fantasies of the Old West. Guests would sleep in cabins, enjoy fine meals at the lodge, and spend their days horseback riding, hunting, and fishing. The growth of these ranches shows an increasing democratization of Jackson's tourist scene, with the previous generation of wilderness pack trip only accessible to the upper crust of Euro-American society. (Courtesy of the American Heritage Center, University of Wyoming.)

MR. AMERICAN CITIZEN:

If you want to feel free to roam at will over 221,610 acres of forests and other recreational areas, as you have been privileged to do in Jackson Hole, prior to the creation of the Jackson Hole National Monument, then will you please sign the enclosed forms and mail them to your Senators and Congressmen.

If this monument is allowed to remain under National Park Service control, your recreational privileges in Jackson Hole will be practically at an end. There will be "don't" signs staring you in the face every mile or less over the entire area.

If the President's authority to create national monuments is not abolished, and such authority returned to Congress, he is liable to make a monument out of YOUR HOME AND FRONT YARD. IT HAPPENED TO US, IT CAN HAPPEN TO YOU!

LET'S BE AMERICANS ONCE MORE!

Jackson Hole Citizens.

This petition, signed by "Jackson Hole Citizens," suggests the controversy following FDR's 1943 declaration of an expanded Jackson Hole National Monument. This declaration did not take any land, it simply combined federal lands in Teton National Forest with a 35,000-acre donation from John D. Rockefeller Jr. Fears about the power of the federal government were, and remain, strong in Wyoming. (Courtesy of the American Heritage Center, University of Wyoming.)

These five fishermen display the bounty they pulled out of Jackson Lake from aboard two boats. The recreational opportunities that drew travelers to Jackson Hole were centered on the ecological and environmental resources of the valley. (Courtesy of the Wyoming State Archives.)

This photograph shows a mounted group in front of Jackson Lake Lodge. Horseback riding has become a vital element in the suite of recreational activities that draws tourists to Jackson for a Western experience, and these folks seem to have been having a good time. (Courtesy of the Wyoming State Archives.)

This aerial shot adds some perspective on the scale of Jackson Lake Lodge. Jackson Lake and the Tetons fill the background, while the lodge's parking lots, roads, and outbuildings crowd the foreground. Postwar development of tourist facilities has always had to walk a fine line between providing the facilities needed for the rush of tourists while also protecting the landscape. (Courtesy of the Wyoming State Archives.)

Here, Wallace Beery is pictured in June 1940 while in the valley to film *Wyoming*. At this time, Beery, an Academy Award winner, was the highest paid actor in the world. Western films shot in Jackson Hole and in other towns like it build connections between actors and viewers and the landscape and mythologized history of the Old West. Beery later moved to Jackson and became a key opponent of the creation of Grand Teton National Park. (Courtesy of the Wyoming State Archives.)

Covered wagons or chuck wagons provide the basis for a picnic in this mid-century photograph. Chuck wagons were used by herders as a means of storing and preparing food for groups of workers. Preparing food for tourists out of chuck wagons allows visitors to connect with that history. (Courtesy of the Wyoming State Archives.)

Ever since artists and photographers accompanied the Hayden Expeditions of the 1870s, Jackson Hole has made for excellent material. In this photograph from 1946, one can see art students working in the shade of awnings along the Snake River north of Jackson. Little did they know that they would become a subject in their own right. (Courtesy of the Wyoming State Archives.)

According to author Donald Hough, "A dude is one who comes in for weeks and months, stays at a dude ranch or something like it, dresses more like a cowhand than a cowhand does, and in a kind of simple minded way tries to fit into the country." This postcard shows a string of horseback riders leaving the Triangle X Ranch beneath the soaring Grand Teton. Ranch stays with all the associated Western recreational opportunities became increasingly popular in the postwar era. (Courtesy of the Wyoming State Archives.)

Wyoming state highway patrolmen are seen in this 1956 shot unloading illegal slot machines slated for destruction outside the Wort Hotel. Jackson's development into a vacation destination and pleasure town has occasionally tempted proprietors to cater to visitors' darker vices. During Prohibition, visitors found it relatively easy to locate a bottle of whiskey for their hunting expedition or pastoral idyll, perhaps establishing a local culture that catered to tourists' needs despite the letter of the law. The policemen all look very pleased with their haul. (Courtesy of the Wyoming State Archives.)

Jackson's Antler Arches, gracing the entrances to the town's central square, are an iconic sight for visitors. The first arch was built in 1953 thanks to fundraising by the Jackson Hole Rotary Club. These visitors from 1960 contemplate crossing the street to the shops opposite the main square. (Courtesy of the Wyoming State Archives.)

Boardwalk sidewalks were originally installed in Western towns to get pedestrians out of the mud and horse manure. Today, they recall that nostalgic era while spiriting tourists between shops. This scene, from the 1960s or 1970s, shows advertisements for whitewater trips, a gift shop, a leather shop, and art galleries. (Courtesy of the Wyoming State Archives.)

Boats bob in Jackson Lake, tied to a dock at Coulter Bay Landing. The number of boats demonstrates the popularity of this kind of motorized excursion. The extent of the lake was expanded with the 1916 completion of a dam, making it a good option for boat cruises. (Courtesy of the Wyoming State Archives.)

This undated photograph from the Carrigen Collection shows a dirt road winding toward the base of the Teton peaks. The opportunity for a little slice of silence has kept visitors returning year after year to these sublime refuges. A ponderosa pine shades the photographer, while other coniferous trees line the road. (Courtesy of the Wyoming State Archives.)

At the corner of Broadway Avenue and King Street, the Hotel Crabtree was a community fixture in Jackson. Built in 1907 as a family home, it was sold two years later and remodeled into a boardinghouse by the Reeds. The Crabtrees took over when Mr. Reed died and Mrs. Reed left the valley. In 1926, the hotel hosted the crown prince and princess of Sweden. Beginning in the 1960s, the building was used for retail shops until it was torn down in the 1990s and replaced by a replica. (Courtesy of the Wyoming State Archives.)

As the postwar visitation boom intensified, new forms of recreation were developed to cater to visitors. Here, the Jackson Hole Golf Course plays host to four players on the fairway, with the Tetons visible in the background. These new forms of recreation increased opportunities for people but also exacerbated the burden placed on the valley's environment. (Courtesy of the Wyoming State Archives.)

Six

SKIING AND POSTWAR EXPANSION

The first skiing in Jackson Hole was just how one would get around the valley when the snow was too deep for pack stock. The sport exploded in popularity after World War II, when veterans who had trained in mountain tactics (including skiing) in the 10th Mountain Division returned to their home ranges. In Jackson, locals were skiing much earlier than this, with the 1920s seeing skiers on the Town Hill, which would become Mount Snow King. In 1926, a local man named Mike O'Neil built a ski jump on the hill. He had earned fame among the skiers of the valley by being among the first to use two poles and making turns, rather than the single pole most pushed between their legs and used to slow down. In 1932, the hill was renamed the Ruth Hanna Simms Ski Hill for a local woman who had donated money for improvements. In 1936, the Civilian Conservation Corps built a hiking and pack stock trail to the summit, and the winter recreation enthusiasts quickly spotted the opportunity. The next year, the Jackson Hole Ski Association was formed under the guidance of Fred Brown, a local skier and mountaineer.

The next year, 1938, the name was changed to Mount Snow King, and it began to take on the look of an organized ski area. In 1939, Neil Rafferty won a contract from the Jackson Hole Club, a local boosters' organization, to develop skiing infrastructure on Snow King. He bought a used cable from an oil-drilling outfit in Casper, ran it up a narrow chute in the forest, and hooked it up to an old Ford. The cable tow ferried skiers to the top of the primitive runs. Rafferty received a lease on municipal property at the base of the hill and a US Forest Service permit to operate the lift.

Winter sports in Jackson got a boost with the 1946 formation of the Jackson Hole Winter Sports Association. The group pooled $40,000 from locals in order to buy an old tramway from a gold mine in Salida and to hire a Denver company to turn it into a ski lift. The improvised tram lifted 8,500 people to the summit in its first year. The improvements continued the next year with the first single chairlift in Wyoming, which also carried 8,500 people in the 1948–1949 season. It was replaced by a double chair with a new cable in 1958.

In 1971, the resort and 60 acres at the base of the mountain were sold to the Western Standard Corporation of nearby Riverton. Subsequent leases from the town and the US Forest Service put it in charge of 375 acres. New additions included the 1978 Rafferty Lift on the east slope, a lease granted for a summer slide, and the 1994 construction of the Cougar triple chairlift, which can move 1,200 skiers an hour. In advance of the 2002 Winter Olympics in Salt Lake City, the ski teams of eight nations warmed up and trained at Snow King.

On the west side of Jackson Hole, on lands that would become the Jackson Hole Mountain Resort, skiing was also deeply ingrained in the culture. In the 1930s, the Teton Ski Club built lifts and developed ski runs on the Idaho side of the Tetons and put rope tows on Signal Mountain, Leek's Canyon, Two Ocean Mountain, Angle Mountain, a hill near Jackson Lake, and a ridge above the Moose-Wilson Road. The flagship peak of the area, Rendezvous Mountain, was first skied by Paul Petzold, Fred Brown, and Paul's brother Curly. Construction began on the resort that would become Jackson Hole in the spring of 1964. Après Vous Mountain was being skied by 1965, and the next year, the Aerial Tram was shuttling 63 people at a time up to the summit of Rendezvous in nine minutes. In 1970, the first national Powder 8 Championship was staged at the resort.

In 1992, Jackson Hole Ski Corporation was sold to the Kemmerer family, who had a century-long interest in Wyoming mining. Four years later, the US Forest Service revised its mountain master plan, downsizing the capacity allowed by the 1981 development plan from 11,500 skiers per day to 7,690. Upgrades to the Thunder Chair and Après Vous, the new Teewinot quad, increased access to beginner and intermediate terrain. The 1990s also saw more development of Teton Village. And by the turn of the millennium, a new system of backcountry gates was allowing skiers access into thousands of more acres of Teton terrain.

Eight-figure infrastructure projects around the Aerial Tram allowed for year-round recreation above Jackson Hole, with summer recreation for paragliders, hikers, and mountain bikers using the expanded Bike Park. It even allows for sightseers just looking for 360-degree Teton views and a ham sandwich from the deli. In 2012, the Mountain Collective was formed, providing a new model of season pass ownership where skiers are allowed a fixed number of days at a variety of different resorts across North America. The popularity of this model has increased the number of recreationalists traveling from out of state and represents only the latest chapter in a story of winter recreation reshaping Jackson.

With the broad, middle-class prosperity that followed the end of World War II into the 1950s and 1960s, more development came to Jackson. It became more than a lonely Wyoming range town, growing first into a logistical hub where one might pass through and get supplies while on a road trip through the national parks. Eventually, Jackson would become a destination all on its own, attracting visitors from all over the world and keeping them in town with a range of fine lodging, eating, and drinking establishments. With time, development, and promotion, upper-class visitors traveling regionally for a ski vacation developed finer tastes and found Jackson businesses ready to cater to them with luxurious accommodations and indulgent services. A visitor walking or driving through Jackson today is confronted with the products of postwar expansion: busy sidewalks, fetching shops, and exclusive restaurants and bars. But that development, and the second-home owners and tourists that it attracts in growing numbers every year, has caused a cost-of-living crisis that has pushed locals out of town and makes it hard—if not impossible—for the employees of the businesses that cater to guests to find a place to live. Jackson is a sleepy Western town no more.

Jackson is also guilty of promoting a Hollywood-built myth of the West. Architecture, design, and attractions are all built to provide an image that the American tourist has come to expect rather than some kind of authentic historicity. Boardwalk sidewalks, false-fronted buildings, and swinging saloon doors are all holdovers from an era when the boosters of Western towns were desperately trying to convey a sense of permanence rather than the fragile outposts of Euro-American colonization that these towns were. Most vestiges of Indigenous life have been wiped from the urban landscape of Jackson, despite the fact that the descendants of Absaroka, Blackfoot, and Shoshone peoples are still here.

This undated photograph from the top of Snow King's double lift shows the town of Jackson blanketed in a fresh coat of snow—a joy to the skiers lucky enough to play in it. The double lift was constructed in 1958 on top of the single lift that had been ferrying skiers since 1947. The single lift was a local favorite, carrying 8,500 people to the summit during its first full season, but the double chair allowed for faster access and the kinds of heart-to-heart conversations that make skiing a community fixture. In order to upgrade to a double chair, a new tower was built at the top and the old cable was replaced. The double lift began hauling passengers in 1959. (Courtesy of the Wyoming State Archives.)

Skis stuck into the snow in front of this cabin would have been a familiar sight in Jackson. When winter shut down travel within the valley, skis became the only way to get around. The man on the right frowns while holding his rifle, and the man on the left smokes a pipe while leaning against the cabin's porch. (S.N. Leek Papers, courtesy of the American Heritage Center, University of Wyoming.)

Seven boys follow their leader on skis in this shot from the 1930s. The generation that would bring skiing facility development to Jackson in the postwar era was the same generation that grew up on skis in the mountains around Jackson in the interwar years. (S.N. Leek Papers, courtesy of the American Heritage Center, University of Wyoming.)

This is an early shot of five boys and one man holding their skis in front of Snow King Mountain. Compare their giant skis, telemark-style bindings, and cold-weather clothing with the high-tech assemblages of gear more familiar on Jackson Hole's slopes today. No doubt they still had fun, based on their smiles. (S.N. Leek Papers, courtesy of the American Heritage Center, University of Wyoming.)

Riding The
SNOW KING MTN
CHAIR LIFT
Jackson. Wyo.
29 AUG 1953
13 708
3 J

This August 1953 picture hints at the recreational opportunities that ski resorts could provide in the summertime. The Tetons rise resolutely behind him, and below, the town of Jackson has taken on a form that modern visitors would recognize. Flat Creek traces the bottom of East Gros Ventre Butte. (Courtesy of the Wyoming State Archives.)

This aerial shot, undated but likely from 1964 or 1965, shows Teton Village under construction at the base of the new Jackson Hole Ski Resort. The large block between the clock tower and lodge is the base of the Aerial Tram. The tram began operations in 1966 and continues to this day, taking nine minutes to shuttle 63 people to the 10,450-foot summit of Rendezvous Mountain. (Courtesy of the Wyoming State Archives.)

A man takes a second out of his ski run to look at the town of Jackson far below, with the entire landscape covered in a fresh coat of snow. Winter may bring its challenges to Jackson, but it, along with the terrain, has made the town a skier's paradise. (Courtesy of the Wyoming State Archives)

The spire of the Jackson Hole Ski Lodge blocks the midday sun as skiers trek to and from the slopes. The Aerial Tram departs uphill behind them for its several-minute run up to the top of the resort. The mid-century construction of facilities such as this lodge allowed for a dramatic expansion in the numbers of people visiting Jackson, boosting the regional economy and impacting the local ecology. (Courtesy of the Wyoming State Archives.)

This shot, taken not long after the 1966 completion of the tram, shows the top tower, where skiers disembark and face the steep slopes below them. Rime ice cakes the tower, a reminder of the harsh conditions that the Teton peaks can deliver up year-round. Skiers have been drawn to this valley's slopes for nearly a century. (Courtesy of the Wyoming State Archives.)

A man unloads a sedan adorned with skis in front of the Alpenhof Lodge, with Jackson Hole Mountain Resort's recognizable clock tower in the background. Visible high above are skiers wending their way downslope, while the towers of the ski lifts stick up like gargantuan trees. This scene dates from 1978. (Courtesy of the Wyoming State Archives.)

A skier in a pig costume—likely not his normal skiing garb—races down the hill toward some kind of slalom flag while spectators cheer him on from above. Silly games, festivities, and displays like this are common in the spring, when the sun is blazing, serious skiing is in the past, and people are looking to have a good time. (Courtesy of the Wyoming State Archives.)

A ski racer stands at the starting gate, poised and ready to go. Three race officials stand by, each with specific duties designed to ensure a fair competition. Ski racing, especially large meets with hundreds of racers, is a specialty of Jackson Hole Mountain Resort and is a boon to the local economy. (Courtesy of the Wyoming State Archives.)

Above, a skier races off the top of Snow King Mountain with the town of Jackson visible behind. At left, skiers make their way down the slopes while others on the chairlift look down at their turns. Scenes like these form the core of many visits to Jackson, especially after the expansion of the region's skiing scene in the 1960s and 1970s. (Both, courtesy of the Wyoming State Archives.)

This photograph is more evidence of springtime goofiness on the slopes, with one man in shorts and the other skiing right up to the advancing line of grass as others look on from behind. Jackson Hole's tram is in the background, standing ready for another trip to the summit. (Courtesy of the Wyoming State Archives.)

This ski racer is seen exploding out of the course's starting gates with a grimace of determination, exuberance, and perhaps a dash of fear on his face. A man in a snowsuit scratches his chin behind him, perhaps contemplating the racer's prospects on the slopes below. (Courtesy of the Wyoming State Archives.)

In the photograph above, a skier flies through the air in his formal attire—a turtleneck and slacks. Below, a coach talks his young charges through the course ahead. The ski slopes around Jackson Hole might over-index on steep-and-deep terrain, but they have also been used to teach generations of kids how to ski. (Both, courtesy of the Wyoming State Archives.)

Those who grew up skiing here and others from farther afield come to Jackson Hole to test their mettle. This skier stays tucked in an aerodynamic crouch as they fly over white snow. In the shot below, the Aerial Tram loads skiers for the quick ride from Teton Village to the summit of Rendezvous Mountain. (Both, courtesy of the Wyoming State Archives.)

Braided ribbons of flags mark out a slalom course as skiers gather on either side to watch. Organized races draw many participants and also increase visibility and interest from other skiers, helping elevate Jackson Hole to the Mount Rushmore of North American ski destinations. (Courtesy of the Wyoming State Archives.)

This 1951 shot shows the front of Utopia Lodge. In the postwar years, Jackson businesses increasingly catered to tourists arriving in their automobiles, and motel facilities such as these grew more popular. While these motels were similar to those found elsewhere in the country, they tried to maintain an authentic local aesthetic and remain similar to Jackson's earliest hotels and boardinghouses. (Finis Mitchell Papers, courtesy of the American Heritage Center, University of Wyoming.)

This photograph shows Pres. John F. Kennedy disembarking at the Jackson Hole Airport on his way to Jackson Hole Lodge. He was greeted by Wyoming senator Gale McGee and a crowd of 3,000 fans. Kennedy's ideas on conservation were shaped by the overindustrialization of the Cape Cod seashore, and he sponsored a bill in 1959 with his Republican counterpart, Sen. Leverett Saltonstall, to establish the Cape Cod National Seashore. One is left to wonder about his impressions of the Jackson Hole landscape and his predecessor's actions that strengthened public protections. (Gale W. McGee Papers, courtesy of the American Heritage Center, University of Wyoming.)

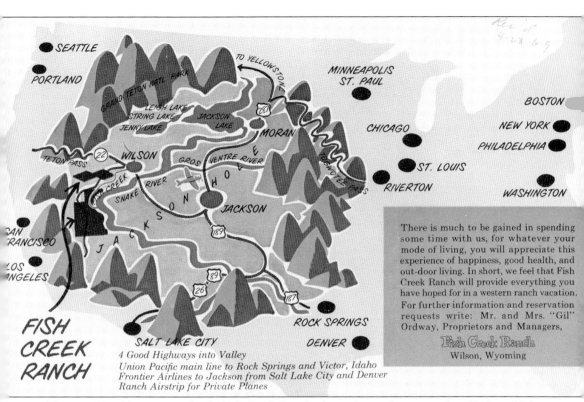

There is much to be gained in spending some time with us, for whatever your mode of living, you will appreciate this experience of happiness, good health, and out-door living. In short, we feel that Fish Creek Ranch will provide everything you have hoped for in a western ranch vacation. For further information and reservation requests write: Mr. and Mrs. "Gil" Ordway, Proprietors and Managers,

Fish Creek Ranch
Wilson, Wyoming

4 Good Highways into Valley
Union Pacific main line to Rock Springs and Victor, Idaho
Frontier Airlines to Jackson from Salt Lake City and Denver
Ranch Airstrip for Private Planes

This travel booklet, put together by Fish Creek Ranch, shows the psychic geography of Jackson Hole, including how boosters pictured the relationship between and isolation from other cities around the country (while maintaining links of mobility for the use of potential visitors). Jackson Hole is imagined as a mountain oasis, shielded on all sides by high mountains yet accessible to tourists via the region's modern highways. (Courtesy of the American Heritage Center, University of Wyoming.)

The mountains surrounding Jackson have always been a draw. This scene, of a person taking a photograph of Snow King Mountain and the town of Jackson far below, could have been last week or a century ago. Americans have been drawn to these landscapes since time immemorial. Jackson's rodeo arena is the expanse of snow in the back right section of town. (Courtesy of the Wyoming State Archives.)

This postcard shot of Jackson's main street from the 1960s is a scene many today would recognize. The Million Dollar Cowboy Bar still stands in the same place, across Highway 191 from Jackson's Town Square, flanked by restaurants and gift shops. (Courtesy of the Wyoming State Archives.)

This image, from a promotional brochure trying to evoke the sights, smells, and sounds of the Old West, shows a man working two big skillets for bacon and pancakes. Behind a wooden fence, the horses stand saddled and ready for the day's rides. The success of dude ranches in the second half of the 20th century has refashioned the historical memory of the Old West. (Courtesy of the Wyoming State Archives.)

This 1970 postcard shows an array of cars and planes parked outside Jackson Hole's airport, with the Tetons looming overhead. It is the only airport in the country situated within the bounds of a national park. Commercial service began in the 1970s, fueling tourism in the valley. (Courtesy of the Wyoming State Archives.)

When the inaugural flight from Frontier Airlines arrived in Jackson Hole, the town had entered a new phase of its development. Now, rather than the arduous overland journeys suffered by potential visitors of previous generations, a traveler could get on a plane in a city anywhere on the continent and disembark several hours later under the lofty peaks of the Tetons. This was good for local businesses catering to visitors but perhaps chipped away at the pride Jacksonites felt about their isolated and rugged valley. Regardless, the town came out to celebrate; a luncheon (above) and a champagne party (below) are pictured, part of the events designed to celebrate Jackson's new link with the wider world. (Both, courtesy of the Wyoming State Archives.)

The interior of the Silver Bar is shown in this 1978 photograph. Positioned right on Broadway, beneath the Wort Hotel, the bar has long been a community institution. It is claimed that one million silver dollars were inlaid in the bar top. (Courtesy of the Wyoming State Archives.)

Jackson's main square and characteristic antler arch are seen on a sunny day in the 2020s. The square is ringed by commercial establishments catering to visitors' every need, while the slopes of Mount Snow King rise above town, greened by a heavy snow pack and wet spring. (Author's collection.)

The exterior doors of the Million Dollar Cowboy Bar face the square, closed to the late morning heat and disappointing would-be revelers until their 11:00 a.m. opening. The bar has hosted visitors and locals alike for eating, drinking, and entertainment since 1937, a centerpiece of the community. (Author's collection.)

Tourists and cars all wait to get through the intersection of Cache Street and Broadway Avenue. During the summer months, the traffic is nonstop as those staying in town try to get food and fun while those trying to get through town fight to get on to the national parks to the north. (Author's collection.)

Built in 1915 and 1916, the Jackson Hole Playhouse is Jackson's oldest surviving building. Visitors today can enjoy a dinner and a show, but in 1920, it would have been the local Ford Model T dealership, and over the years, the building has served as a bowling alley, post office, and mercantile store. (Author's collection.)

Jackson has retained its signature boardwalk sidewalks around the main square, a callback to the town's frontier origins, when mud and manure would have blanketed the streets and pathways in several inches of muck. The town's relationship with its Wild West past is complicated, with the darker chapters papered over and a marketing campaign that prizes tourists' nostalgia over historical accuracy. (Author's collection.)

This photograph shows the intersection of Cache Street and Broadway Avenue with cars from all over the country lined up to head north toward the national parks. Modern Jackson's genesis can be traced to the mid-20th century's growing flood of road trippers who tied the town to the nearby national parks and ski resorts. (Author's collection.)

BIBLIOGRAPHY

Betts, Robert B. *Along the Ramparts of the Tetons: The Saga of Jackson Hole, Wyoming.* Niwot: University Press of Colorado, 1978.

Huidekoper, Virginia. *The Early Days in Jackson Hole.* 5th printing. Moose, WY: Grand Teton Natural History Association, 1997.

Layser, Earl F. *The Jackson Hole Settlement Chronicles: The Lives and Times of the First Settlers.* Alta, WY: Dancing Pine Publishing, 2012.

Nelson, Fern K. *This Was Jackson's Hole: Incidents and Profiles from the Settlement of Jackson Hole.* Glendo, WY: High Plains Press, 1994.

Starr, Eileen F. *Architecture in the Cowboy State, 1849–1940: A Guide.* Glendo, WY: High Plains Press, 1992.

Wilson, R. Michael. *Outlaw Tales of Wyoming: True Stories of the Cowboy State's Most Infamous Crooks, Culprits, and Cutthroats.* 2nd ed. Helena, MT: Twodot, 2013.

DISCOVER THOUSANDS OF LOCAL HISTORY BOOK
FEATURING MILLIONS OF VINTAGE IMAGES

Arcadia Publishing, the leading local history publisher in the United States, is committed to making history accessible and meaningful through publishing books that celebrate and preserve the heritage of America's people and places.

Find more books like this at
www.arcadiapublishing.com

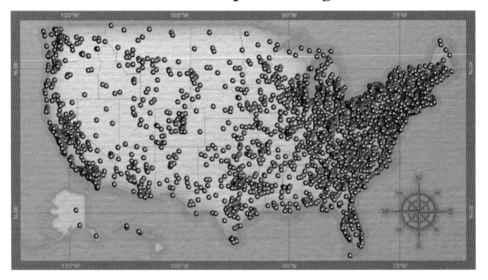

Search for your hometown history, your old stomping grounds, and even your favorite sports team.

Consistent with our mission to preserve history on a local level, this book was printed in South Carolina on American-made paper and manufactured entirely in the United States. Products carrying the accredited Forest Stewardship Council (FSC) label are printed on 100 percent FSC-certified paper.

MADE IN THE USA